THE OLDEST CODE OF LAWS
IN THE WORLD

Hammurabi, king of Babylonia.

THE

OLDEST CODE OF LAWS
IN THE WORLD

THE CODE OF LAWS PROMULGATED BY
HAMMURABI, KING OF BABYLON
B.C. 2285–2242

TRANSLATED

BY

C. H. W. JOHNS, M.A. 1857-1920

LECTURER IN ASSYRIOLOGY, QUEENS' COLLEGE, CAMBRIDGE
AUTHOR OF "ASSYRIAN DEEDS AND DOCUMENTS"
"AN ASSYRIAN DOOMSDAY BOOK"

EDINBURGH
T. & T. CLARK, 38 GEORGE STREET
1903

PRINTED BY
MORRISON AND GIBB LIMITED

FOR

T. & T. CLARK, EDINBURGH

LONDON : SIMPKIN, MARSHALL, HAMILTON, KENT, AND CO. LIMITED
NEW YORK : CHARLES SCRIBNER'S SONS

INTRODUCTION

———+———

THE Code of Ḫammurabi is one of the most
important monuments in the history of the
human race. Containing as it does the laws
which were enacted by a king of Babylonia in
the third millennium B.C., whose rule extended
over the whole of Mesopotamia from the
mouths of the rivers Tigris and Euphrates to
the Mediterranean coast, we must regard it
with interest. But when we reflect that the
ancient Hebrew tradition ascribed the migra-
tion of Abraham from Ur of the Chaldees
to this very period, and clearly means to
represent their tribe father as triumphing
over this very same Ḫammurabi (Amraphel,
Gen. xiv. 1), we can hardly doubt that
these very laws were part of that tradition.
At any rate, they must have served to

mould and fix the ideas of right throughout
that great empire, and so form the state of
society in Canaan when, five hundred years
later, the Hebrews began to dominate that
region.

Such was the effect produced on the minds
of succeeding generations by this superb codi-
fication of the judicial decisions of past ages,
which had come to be regarded as 'the
right,' that two thousand years and more
later it was made a text-book for study in the
schools of Babylonia, being divided for that
purpose into some twelve chapters, and en-
titled, after the Semitic custom, *Ninu ilu
sirum*, from its opening words. In Assyria
also, in the seventh century B.C., it was studied
in a different edition, apparently under the
name of 'The Judgments of Righteousness
which Hammurabi, the great king, set up.'
These facts point to it as certain to affect
Jewish views before and after the Exile, in a
way that we may expect to find as funda-
mental as the Babylonian influence in cos-
mology or religion.

For many years fragments have been

known, have been studied, and from internal
evidence ascribed to the period of the first
dynasty of Babylon, even called by the name
Code Ḥammurabi. It is just cause for pride
that Assyriology, so young a science as only
this year to have celebrated the centenary of
its birth, is able to emulate astronomy and
predict the discovery of such bright stars as
this. But while we certainly should have
directed our telescopes to Babylonia for the
rising of this light from the East, it was
really in Elam, at Susa, the old Persepolis,
that the find was made. The Elamites were
the great rivals of Babylonia for centuries,
and it seems likely that some Elamite conqueror carried off the stone from a temple at
Sippara, in Babylonia.

However that may be, we owe it to the
French Government, who have been carrying
on explorations at Susa for years under the
superintendence of M. J. de Morgan, that a
monument, only disinterred in January, has
been copied, transcribed, translated, and
published, in a superb quarto volume, by
October. The ancient text is reproduced by

photogravure in a way that enables a student to verify word by word what the able editor, Father V. Scheil, *Professeur à l'École des Hautes-Études*, has given as his reading of the archaic signs. The volume, which appears as *Tome IV., Textes Élamites-Sémitiques*, of the *Mémoires de la Délégation en Perse* (Paris, Leroux, 1902), is naturally rather expensive for the ordinary reader. Besides, the rendering of the eminent French savant, while distinguished by that clear, neat phrasing which is so charming a feature of all his work, is often rather a paraphrase than a translation. The ordinary reader who desires to estimate for himself the importance of the new monument will be forced to wonder how and why the same word in the original gets such different renderings. Prolonged study will be needed to bring out fully the whole meaning of many passages, and it may conduce to such a result to present the public with an alternative rendering in an English dress. Needless to say, scholars will continue to use Scheil's edition as the ultimate source, but for comparative purposes a literal translation may be welcome as an introduction.

The monument itself consists of a block of black diorite, nearly eight feet high, found in pieces, but readily rejoined. It contains on the obverse a very interesting representation of the King Ḫammurabi, receiving his laws from the seated sun-god Šamaš, ' the judge of heaven and earth.' Then follow, on the obverse, sixteen columns of writing with 1114 lines. There were five more columns on this side, but they have been erased and the stone repolished, doubtless by the Elamite conqueror, who meant to inscribe his name and titles there. As we have lost those five columns we may regret that he did not actually do this, but there is now no trace of any hint as to who carried off the stone. On the reverse side are twenty-eight columns with more than 2500 lines of inscription.

A great space, some 700 lines, is devoted by the king to setting out his titles, his glory, his care for his subjects, his veneration of his gods, and incidentally revealing the cities and districts under his rule, with many interesting hints as to local cults. He also invokes blessing on those who should preserve and respect his monument, and curses those who should injure or remove it. A translation of this portion is not given, as it is unintelligible without copious comment and is quite foreign to the purpose of this book, which aims solely at making the Code intelligible.

I desire to express my obligations to Dr. F. Carr for his many kind suggestions as to the meaning of the Code.

The Index will, it is hoped, serve more or less as a digest of the Code. One great difficulty of any translation of a law document must always be that the technical expressions of one language cannot be rendered in terms that are co-extensive. The rendering will have implications foreign to the original. An attempt to minimise misconceptions is made by suggesting alternative renderings in the Index. Further, by labelling a certain section, as the law of incest, for example, one definitely fixes the sense in which the translation is to be read. Hence it is hoped that the Index will be no less helpful than the translation in giving readers an idea of what the Code really meant.

No doubt this remarkable monument will be made the subject of many valuable monographs in the future, which will greatly elucidate passages now obscure. But it was thought that the interest of the subject warranted an immediate issue of an English translation, which would place the chief features of the Code before a wider public than those who could read the original. The present translation is necessarily tentative in many places, but it is hoped marks an advance over those already published.

Dr. H. Winckler's rendering of the Code came into my hands after this work was sent to the publishers, and I have not thought it necessary to withdraw any of my renderings. In some points he has improved upon Professor Scheil's work, in other points he is scarcely so good. But any discussion is not in place here. I gratefully acknowledge my obligations to both, but have used an independent judgment all through. I hope shortly to set out my reasons for the differences between us in a larger work. A few of Dr. Winckler's renderings are quoted in the Index, and marked—Winckler's tr.

C. H. W. JOHNS.

Cambridge,
January 31, 1903.

THE OLDEST CODE OF LAWS IN THE WORLD

THE TEXT OF THE CODE

§ 1. IF a man weave a spell and put a ban upon a man, and has not justified himself, he that wove the spell upon him shall be put to death.

§ 2. If a man has put a spell upon a man, and has not justified himself, he upon whom the spell is laid shall go to the holy river, he shall plunge into the holy river, and if the holy river overcome him, he who wove the spell upon him shall take to himself his house. If the holy river makes that man to be innocent, and has saved him, he who laid the spell upon him shall be put to death. He who plunged into the holy river shall take to himself the house of him who wove the spell upon him.

§ 3. If a man, in a case pending judgement, has uttered threats against the witnesses, or has not justified the word that he has spoken, if that case be a capital suit, that man shall be put to death.

§ 4. If he has offered corn or money to the witnesses, he shall himself bear the sentence of that case.

§ 5. If a judge has judged a judgement, decided a decision, granted a sealed sentence, and afterwards has altered his judgement, that judge, for the alteration of the judgement that he judged, one shall put him to account, and he shall pay twelvefold the penalty which was in the said judgement, and in the assembly one shall expel him from his judgement seat, and he shall not return, and with the judges at a judgement he shall not take his seat.

§ 6. If a man has stolen the goods of temple or palace, that man shall be killed, and he who has received the stolen thing from his hand shall be put to death.

§ 7. If a man has bought silver, gold, manservant or maidservant, ox or sheep or ass, or anything whatever its name, from the hand of a man's son, or of a man's slave, without witness and bonds, or has received the same on deposit, that man has acted the thief, he shall be put to death.

§ 8. If a man has stolen ox or sheep or ass, or pig, or ship, whether from the temple or the palace, he shall pay thirtyfold. If he be a poor man, he shall render tenfold. If the thief has nought to pay, he shall be put to death.

§ 9. If a man who has lost something of his, something of his that is lost has been seized in the hand of a man, the man in whose hand the lost thing has been seized has said, 'A giver gave it me,' or 'I bought it before witnesses,' and the owner of the thing that is lost has said, 'Verily, I will bring witnesses that know my lost property,' the buyer has brought the giver who gave it him and the witnesses before whom he bought it, and the owner of the lost property has brought the witnesses who know his lost property, the judge shall see their depositions, the witnesses before whom the purchase was made and the witnesses knowing the lost property shall say out before God what they know; and if the giver has acted the thief he shall be put to death, the owner of the lost property shall take his lost property, the buyer shall take the money he paid from the house of the giver.

§ 10. If the buyer has not brought the giver who gave it him and the witnesses before whom he bought, and the owner of the lost property has brought the witnesses knowing his lost property, the buyer has acted the thief, he shall be put to death; the owner of the lost property shall take his lost property.

§ 11. If the owner of the lost property has not brought witnesses knowing his lost property, he has lied, he has stirred up strife, he shall be put to death.

§ 12. If the giver has betaken himself to

his fate, the buyer shall take from the house of the giver fivefold as the penalty of that case.

§ 13. If that man has not his witnesses near, the judge shall set him a fixed time, up to six months, and if within six months he has not driven in his witnesses, that man has lied, he himself shall bear the blame of that case.

§ 14. If a man has stolen the son of a freeman, he shall be put to death.

§ 15. If a man has caused either a palace slave or palace maid, or a slave of a poor man or a poor man's maid, to go out of the gate, he shall be put to death.

§ 16. If a man has harboured in his house a manservant or a maidservant, fugitive from the palace, or a poor man, and has not produced them at the demand of the commandant, the owner of that house shall be put to death.

§ 17. If a man has captured either a manservant or a maidservant, a fugitive, in the open country and has driven him back to his master, the owner of the slave shall pay him two shekels of silver.

§ 18. If that slave will not name his owner he shall drive him to the palace, and one shall enquire into his past, and cause him to return to his owner.

§ 19. If he confine that slave in his house, and afterwards the slave has been seized in his hand, that man shall be put to death.

§ 20. If the slave has fled from the hand of his captor, that man shall swear by the name of God, to the owner of the slave, and shall go free.

§ 21. If a man has broken into a house, one shall kill him before the breach and bury him in it (?).

§ 22. If a man has carried on brigandage, and has been captured, that man shall be put to death.

§ 23. If the brigand has not been caught, the man who has been despoiled shall recount before God what he has lost, and the city and governor in whose land and district the

brigandage took place shall render back to
him whatever of his was lost.

§ 24. If it was a life, the city and governor
shall pay one mina of silver to his people.

§ 25. If in a man's house a fire has been
kindled, and a man who has come to ex-
tinguish the fire has lifted up his eyes to
the property of the owner of the house, and
has taken the property of the owner of the
house, that man shall be thrown into that
fire.

§ 26. If either a ganger or a constable,
whose going on an errand of the king has
been ordered, goes not, or hires a hireling and
sends him in place of himself, that ganger or
constable shall be put to death; his hireling
shall take to himself his house.

§ 27. If a ganger or a constable, who is
diverted to the fortresses of the king, and
after him one has given his field and his
garden to another, and he has carried on his
business, if he returns and regains his city, one
shall return to him his field and his garden,
and he shall carry on his business himself.

§ 28. If a ganger or a constable who is diverted to the fortresses of the king, his son be able to carry on the business, one shall give him field and garden and he shall carry on his father's business.

§ 29. If his son is young and is not able to carry on his father's business, one-third of the field and garden shall be given to his mother, and his mother shall rear him.

§ 30. If a ganger or a constable has left alone his field, or his garden, or his house, from the beginning of his business, and has caused it to be waste, a second after him has taken his field, his garden, or his house, and has gone about his business for three years, if he returns and regains his city, and would cultivate his field, his garden, and his house, one shall not give them to him ; he who has taken them and carried on his business shall carry it on.

§ 31. If it is one year only and he had let it go waste, and he shall return, one shall give his field, his garden, and his house, and he shall carry on his business.

§ 32. If a ganger or a constable who is diverted on an errand of the king's, a merchant has ransomed him and caused him to regain his city, if in his house there is means for his ransom, he shall ransom his own self; if in his house there is no means for his ransom, he shall be ransomed from the temple of his city; if in the temple of his city there is not means for his ransom, the palace shall ransom him. His field, his garden, and his house shall not be given for his ransom.

§ 33. If either a governor or a magistrate has taken to himself the men of the levy, or has accepted and sent on the king's errand a hired substitute, that governor or magistrate shall be put to death.

§ 34. If either a governor or a magistrate has taken to himself the property of a ganger, has plundered a ganger, has given a ganger to hire, has stolen from a ganger in a judgement by high-handedness, has taken to himself the gift the king has given the ganger, that governor or magistrate shall be put to death.

§ 35. If a man has bought the cattle or

sheep which the king has given to the ganger from the hand of the ganger, he shall be deprived of his money.

§ 36. The field, garden, and house of a ganger, or constable, or a tributary, he shall not give for money.

§ 37. If a man has bought the field, garden, or house of a ganger, a constable, or a tributary, his tablet shall be broken and he shall be deprived of his money. The field, garden, or house he shall return to its owner.

§ 38. The ganger, constable, or tributary shall not write off to his wife, or his daughter, from the field, garden, or house of his business, and he shall not assign it for his debt.

§ 39. From the field, garden, and house which he has bought and acquired, he may write off to his wife or his daughter and give for his debt.

§ 40. A votary, merchant, or foreign sojourner may sell his field, his garden, or his house; the buyer shall carry on the business of the field, garden, or house which he has bought.

§ 41. If a man has bartered for the field, garden, or house of a ganger, constable, or tributary, and has given exchanges, the ganger, constable, or tributary shall return to his field, garden, or house, and shall keep the exchanges given him.

§ 42. If a man has taken a field to cultivate and has not caused the corn to grow in the field, and has not done the entrusted work on the field, one shall put him to account and he shall give corn like its neighbour.

§ 43. If he has not cultivated the field and has left it to itself, he shall give corn like its neighbour to the owner of the field, and the field he left he shall break up with hoes and shall harrow it and return to the owner of the field.

§ 44. If a man has taken on hire an unreclaimed field for three years to open out, and has left it aside, has not opened the field, in the fourth year he shall break it up with hoes, he shall hoe it, and harrow it, and return to the owner of the field, and he shall measure out ten GUR of corn per GAN.

§ 45. If a man has given his field for produce to a cultivator, and has received the produce of his field, and afterwards a thunderstorm has ravaged the field or carried away the produce, the loss is the cultivator's.

§ 46. If he has not received the produce of his field, and has given the field either for one-half or for one-third, the corn that is in the field the cultivator and the owner of the field shall share according to the tenour of their contract.

§ 47. If the cultivator, because in the former year he did not set up his dwelling, has assigned the field to cultivation, the owner of the field shall not condemn the cultivator; his field has been cultivated, and at harvest time he shall take corn according to his bonds.

§ 48. If a man has a debt upon him and a thunderstorm ravaged his field or carried away the produce, or the corn has not grown through lack of water, in that year he shall not return corn to the creditor, he shall alter his tablet and he shall not give interest for that year.

§ 49. If a man has taken money from a merchant and has given to the merchant a field planted with corn or sesame, and said to him, 'Cultivate the field, reap and take for thyself the corn and sesame which there is,' if the cultivator causes to grow corn or sesame in the field, at the time of harvest the owner of the field forsooth shall take the corn or sesame which is in the field and shall give corn for the money which he took from the merchant, and for its interests and for the dwelling of the cultivator, to the merchant.

§ 50. If the field was cultivated or the field of sesame was cultivated when he gave it, the owner of the field shall take the corn or sesame which is in the field and shall return the money and its interests to the merchant.

§ 51. If he has not money to return, the sesame, according to its market price for the money and its interest which he took from the merchant, according to the standard fixed by the king, he shall give to the merchant.

§ 52. If the cultivator has not caused corn or sesame to grow in the field, he shall not alter his bonds.

§ 53. If a man has neglected to strengthen his bank of the canal, has not strengthened his bank, a breach has opened out itself in his bank, and the waters have carried away the meadow, the man in whose bank the breach has been opened shall render back the corn which he has caused to be lost.

§ 54. If he is not able to render back the corn, one shall give him and his goods for money, and the people of the meadow whose corn the water has carried away shall share it.

§ 55. If a man has opened his runnel to water and has neglected it, and the field of his neighbour the waters have carried away, he shall pay corn like his neighbour.

§ 56. If a man has opened the waters, and the plants of the field of his neighbour the waters have carried away, he shall pay ten *GUR* of corn *per GAN*.

§ 57. If a shepherd has caused the sheep to feed on the green corn, has not come to an agreement with the owner of the field, without the consent of the owner of the field has made the sheep feed off the field, the owner shall reap his fields, the shepherd who without consent of the owner of the field has fed off the field with sheep shall give over and above twenty *GUR* of corn *per GAN* to the owner of the field.

§ 58. If from the time that the sheep have gone up from the meadow, and the whole flock has passed through the gate, the shepherd has laid his sheep on the field and has caused the sheep to feed off the field, the shepherd who has made them feed off the field one shall watch, and at harvest time he shall measure out sixty *GUR* of corn *per GAN* to the owner of the field.

§ 59. If a man without the consent of the owner of the orchard has cut down a tree in a man's orchard, he shall pay half a mina of silver.

§ 60. If a man has given a field to a gardener to plant a garden and the gardener has planted the garden, four years he shall rear the garden, in the fifth year the owner of the garden and the gardener shall share equally, the owner of the garden shall cut off his share and take it.

§ 61. If the gardener has not included all the field in the planting, has left a waste place, he shall set the waste place in the share which he takes.

§ 62. If the field which has been given him to plant he has not planted as a garden, if it was corn land, the gardener shall measure out corn to the owner of the field, like its neighbour, as produce of the field for the years that are neglected, and he shall do the ordered work on the field and return to the owner of the field.

§ 63. If the field was unreclaimed land, he shall do the ordered work on the field and return it to the owner of the field and measure out ten *GUR* of corn *per GAN* for each year.

§ 64. If a man has given his garden to a

gardener to farm, the gardener as long as he holds the garden shall give to the owner of the garden two-thirds from the produce of the garden, and he himself shall take one-third.

§ 65. If the gardener does not farm the garden and has diminished the yield, he shall measure out the yield of the garden like its neighbour.

NOTE.—Here five columns of the monument have been erased, only the commencing characters of column xvii. being visible. The subjects of this last part included the further enactments concerning the rights and duties of gardeners, the whole of the regulations concerning houses let to tenants, and the relationships of the merchant to his agents, which continue on the obverse of the monument. [See page 58.] Scheil estimates the lost portion at 35 sections, and following him we recommence with

§ 100. . . . the interests of the money, as much as he took, he shall write down, and when he has numbered his days he shall answer his merchant.

2

§ 101. If where he has gone he has not seen prosperity, he shall make up and return the money he took, and the agent shall give to the merchant.

§ 102. If a merchant has given to the agent money as a favour, and where he has gone he has seen loss, the full amount of money he shall return to the merchant.

§ 103. If while he goes on his journey the enemy has made him quit whatever he was carrying, the agent shall swear by the name of God and shall go free.

§ 104. If the merchant has given to the agent corn, wool, oil, or any sort of goods, to traffic with, the agent shall write down the price and hand over to the merchant; the agent shall take a sealed memorandum of the price which he shall give to the merchant.

§ 105. If an agent has forgotten and has not taken a sealed memorandum of the money he has given to the merchant, money that is not sealed for, he shall not put in his accounts.

§ 106. If an agent has taken money from a

merchant and his merchant has disputed with him, that merchant shall put the agent to account before God and witnesses concerning the money taken, and the agent shall give to the merchant the money as much as he has taken threefold.

§ 107. If a merchant has wronged an agent and the agent has returned to his merchant whatever the merchant gave him, the merchant has disputed with the agent as to what the agent gave him, that agent shall put the merchant to account before God and witnesses, and the merchant because he disputed the agent shall give to the agent whatever he has taken sixfold.

§ 108. If a wine merchant has not received corn as the price of drink, has received silver by the great stone, and has made the price of drink less than the price of corn, that wine merchant one shall put her to account and throw her into the water.

§ 109. If a wine merchant has collected a riotous assembly in her house and has not seized those rioters and driven them to the

palace, that wine merchant shall be put to
death.

§ 110. If a votary, a lady, who is not living
in the convent, has opened a wine shop or
has entered a wine shop for drink, that
woman one shall burn her.

§ 111. If a wine merchant has given sixty
ḲA of best beer at harvest time for thirst,
she shall take fifty ḲA of corn.

§ 112. If a man stays away on a journey
and has given silver, gold, precious stones,
or treasures of his hand to a man, has caused
him to take them for transport, and that
man whatever was for transport, where he
has transported has not given and has taken
to himself, the owner of the transported
object, that man, concerning whatever he had
to transport and gave not, shall put him to
account, and that man shall give to the owner
of the transported object fivefold whatever
was given him.

§ 113. If a man has corn or money upon a
man, and without consent of the owner of the
corn has taken corn from the heap or from

the store, that man for taking of the corn without consent of the owner of the corn from the heap or from the store, one shall put him to account, and he shall return the corn as much as he has taken, and shall lose all that he gave whatever it be.

§ 114. If a man has not corn or money upon a man and levies a distraint, for every single distraint he shall pay one-third of a mina.

§ 115. If a man has corn or money upon a man and has levied a distraint, and the distress in the house of his distrainer dies a natural death, that case has no penalty.

§ 116. If the distress has died in the house of his distrainer, of blows or of want, the owner of the distress shall put his merchant to account, and if he be the son of a free-man (that has died), his son one shall kill; if the slave of a free-man, he shall pay one-third of a mina of silver, and he shall lose all that he gave whatever it be.

§ 117. If a man a debt has seized him, and he has given his wife, his son, his daughter for the money, or has handed over to work off the debt, for three years they shall work in the house of their buyer or exploiter, in the fourth year he shall fix their liberty.

§ 118. If he has handed over a man-servant or a maidservant to work off a debt, and the merchant shall remove and sell them for money, no one can object.

§ 119. If a debt has seized a man, and he has handed over for the money a maid-servant who has borne him children, the money the merchant paid him the owner of the maid shall pay, and he shall ransom his maid.

§ 120. If a man has heaped up his corn in a heap in the house of a man, and in the granary a disaster has taken place, or the owner of the house has opened the granary and taken the corn, or has disputed as to the total amount of the corn that was heaped up in his house, the owner of the corn shall re-count his corn before God, the owner of the house shall make up and return the corn which he took and shall give to the owner of the corn.

§ 121. If a man has heaped up corn in the house of a man, he shall give as the price of storage five KA of corn *per* GUR of corn *per annum.*

§ 122. If a man shall give silver, gold, or anything whatever, to a man on deposit, all whatever he shall give he shall shew to witnesses and fix bonds and shall give on deposit.

§ 123. If without witness and bonds he has given on deposit, and where he has deposited they keep disputing him, this case has no remedy.

§ 124. If a man has given silver, gold, or anything whatever to a man on deposit before witnesses and he has disputed with him, one shall put that man to account, and whatever he has disputed he shall make up and shall give.

§ 125. If a man has given anything of his on deposit, and where he gave it, either by housebreaking or by rebellion, something of his has been lost, along with something of the owner of the house, the owner of the house who has defaulted all that was given him on deposit and has been lost, he shall make good and render to the owner of the goods, the owner of the house shall seek out whatever of his is lost and take it from the thief.

§ 126. If a man has lost nothing of his, but has said that something of his is lost, has exaggerated his loss, since nothing of his is lost, his loss he shall recount before God, and whatever he has claimed he shall make up and shall give to his loss.

§ 127. If a man has caused the finger to be pointed against a votary, or a man's wife and has not justified himself, that man they shall throw down before the judge and brand his forehead.

§ 128. If a man has married a wife and has not laid down her bonds, that woman is no wife.

§ 129. If the wife of a man has been caught in lying with another male, one shall bind them and throw them into the waters. If the owner of the wife would save his

wife or the king would save his servant (he
may).

§ 130. If a man has forced the wife of a
man who has not known the male and is
dwelling in the house of her father, and has
lain in her bosom and one has caught him,
that man shall be killed, the woman herself
shall go free.

§ 131. If the wife of a man her husband has accused her, and she has not been
caught in lying with another male, she
shall swear by God and shall return to her
house.

§ 132. If a wife of a man on account of
another male has had the finger pointed at
her, and has not been caught in lying with
another male, for her husband she shall plunge
into the holy river.

§ 133. If a man has been taken captive
and in his house there is maintenance, his
wife has gone out from her house and entered
into the house of another, because that
woman has not guarded her body, and has
entered into the house of another, one shall

put that woman to account and throw her into the waters.

§ 134. If a man has been taken captive and in his house there is no maintenance, and his wife has entered into the house of another, that woman has no blame.

§ 135. If a man has been taken captive and in his house there is no maintenance before her, his wife has entered into the house of another and has borne children, afterwards her husband has returned and regained his city, that woman shall return to her bridegroom, the children shall go after their father.

§ 136. If a man has left his city and fled, after him his wife has entered the house of another, if that man shall return and has seized his wife, because he hated his city and fled, the wife of the truant shall not return to her husband.

§ 137. If a man has set his face to put away his concubine who has borne him children or his wife who has granted him children, to that woman he shall return her her marriage portion and shall give her the usufruct of field, garden, and goods, and she shall bring up her children. From the time that her children are grown up, from whatever is given to her children they shall give her a share like that of one son, and she shall marry the husband of her choice.

§ 138. If a man has put away his bride who has not borne him children, he shall give her money as much as her dowry, and shall pay her the marriage portion which she brought from her father's house, and shall put her away.

§ 139. If there was no dowry, he shall give her one mina of silver for a divorce.

§ 140. If he is a poor man, he shall give her one-third of a mina of silver.

§ 141. If the wife of a man who is living in the house of her husband has set her face to go out and has acted the fool, has wasted her house, has belittled her husband, one shall put her to account, and if her husband has said, 'I put her away,' he shall put her away and she shall go her way, he shall not give her anything for her divorce. If her husband has not said 'I put her away,' her husband shall marry another woman, that woman as a maid-servant shall dwell in the house of her husband.

§ 142. If a woman hates her husband and has said 'Thou shalt not possess me,' one shall enquire into her past what is her lack, and if she has been economical and has no vice, and her husband has gone out and greatly belittled her, that woman has no blame, she shall take her marriage portion and go off to her father's house.

§ 143. If she has not been economical, a goer about, has wasted her house, has belittled her husband, that woman one shall throw her into the waters.

§ 144. If a man has espoused a votary, and that votary has given a maid to her husband and has brought up children, that man has set his face to take a concubine, one shall not countenance that man, he shall not take a concubine.

§ 145. If a man has espoused a votary, and she has not granted him children and he has set his face to take a concubine, that man shall take a concubine, he shall cause her to enter into his house. That concubine he shall not put on an equality with the wife.

§ 146. If a man has espoused a votary, and she has given a maid to her husband and she has borne children, afterwards that maid has made herself equal with her mistress, because she has borne children her mistress shall not sell her for money, she shall put a mark upon her and count her among the maidservants.

§ 147. If she has not borne children her mistress may sell her for money.

§ 148. If a man has married a wife and a sickness has seized her, he has set his face to marry a second wife, he may marry her, his wife whom the sickness has seized he shall not put her away, in the home she shall dwell, and as long as she lives he shall sustain her.

§ 149. If that woman is not content to dwell in the house of her husband, he shall pay her her marriage portion which she brought from her father's house, and she shall go off.

§ 150. If a man to his wife has set aside field, garden, house, or goods, has left her a sealed deed, after her husband her children shall not dispute her, the mother after her to her children whom she loves shall give, to brothers she shall not give.

§ 151. If a woman, who is dwelling in the house of a man, her husband has bound himself that she shall not be seized on account of a creditor of her husband's, has granted a deed, if that man before he married that woman had a debt upon him, the creditor shall not seize his wife, and if that woman before she entered the man's house had a debt upon her, her creditor shall not seize her husband.

§ 152. If from the time that that woman entered into the house of the man a debt has come upon them, both together they shall answer the merchant.

§ 153. If a man's wife on account of another male has caused her husband to be killed, that woman upon a stake one shall set her.

§ 154. If a man has known his daughter, that man one shall expel from the city.

§ 155. If a man has betrothed a bride to his son and his son has known her, and he afterwards has lain in her bosom and one has caught him, that man one shall bind and cast her into the waters.

§ 156. If a man has betrothed a bride to his son and his son has not known her, and he has lain in her bosom, he shall pay her half a mina of silver and shall pay to her whatever she brought from her father's house, and she shall marry the husband of her choice.

§ 157. If a man, after his father, has lain in the bosom of his mother, one shall burn them both of them together.

§ 158. If a man, after his father, has been caught in the bosom of her that brought him up, who has borne children, that man shall be cut off from his father's house.

§ 159. If a man who has brought in a present to the house of his father-in-law, has given a dowry, has looked upon another woman, and has said to his father-in-law, 'Thy daughter I will not marry,' the father of the daughter shall take to himself all that he brought him.

§ 160. If a man has brought in a present to the house of his father-in-law, has given a dowry, and the father of the daughter has said, 'My daughter I will not give thee,' he shall make up and return everything that he brought him.

§ 161. If a man has brought in a present to the house of his father-in-law, has given a dowry, and a comrade of his has slandered him, his father-in-law has said to the claimant of the wife, 'My daughter thou shalt not espouse,' he shall make up and return all that he brought him, and his comrade shall not marry his wife.

§ 162. If a man has married a wife and she has borne him children, and that woman has gone to her fate, her father shall have no claim on her marriage portion, her marriage portion is her children's forsooth.

§ 163. If a man has married a wife, and she has not granted him children, that woman has gone to her fate, if his father-in-law has re-

THE TEXT OF THE CODE

turned him the dowry that that man brought
to the house of his father-in-law, her husband
shall have no claim on the marriage portion
of that woman, her marriage portion belongs
to the house of her father forsooth.

§ 164. If his father-in-law has not returned
him the dowry, he shall deduct all her dowry
from his marriage portion and shall return
her marriage portion to the house of her
father.

§ 165. If a man has apportioned to his son,
the first in his eyes, field, garden, and house,
has written him a sealed deed, after the father
has gone to his fate, when the brothers divide,
the present his father gave him he shall take,
and over and above he shall share equally in
the goods of the father's house.

§ 166. If a man, in addition to the children
which he has possessed, has taken a wife, for
his young son has not taken a wife, after the
father has gone to his fate, when the brothers
divide, from the goods of the father's house
to their young brother who has not taken a
wife, beside his share, they shall assign him

3

money as a dowry and shall cause him to take a wife.

§ 167. If a man has taken a wife, and she has borne him sons, that woman has gone to her fate, after her, he has taken to himself another woman and she has borne children, afterwards the father has gone to his fate, the children shall not share according to their mothers, they shall take the marriage portions of their mothers and shall share the goods of their father's house equally.

§ 168. If a man has set his face to cut off his son, has said to the judge 'I will cut off my son,' the judge shall enquire into his reasons, and if the son has not committed a heavy crime which cuts off from sonship, the father shall not cut off his son from sonship.

§ 169. If he has committed against his father a heavy crime which cuts off from son-ship, for the first time the judge shall bring back his face; if he has committed a heavy crime for the second time, the father shall cut off his son from sonship.

§ 170. If a man his wife has borne him

sons, and his maidservant has borne him sons,
the father in his lifetime has said to the sons
which the maidservant has borne him 'my
sons,' has numbered them with the sons of
his wife, after the father has gone to his fate,
the sons of the wife and the sons of the maidservant shall share equally in the goods of the
father's house ; the sons that are sons of the
wife at the sharing shall choose and take.

§ 171. And if the father in his lifetime,
to the sons which the maidservant bore him,
has not said 'my sons,' after the father
has gone to his fate the sons of the maid
shall not share with the sons of the wife in
the goods of the father's house, one shall
assign the maidservant and her sons freedom;
the sons of the wife shall have no claim on
the sons of the maidservant for servitude, the
wife shall take her marriage portion and the
settlement which her husband gave her and
wrote in a deed for her and shall dwell in the
dwelling of her husband, as long as lives she
shall enjoy, for money she shall not give, after
her they are her sons' forsooth.

§ 172. If her husband did not give her a settlement, one shall pay her her marriage portion, and from the goods of her husband's house she shall take a share like one son. If her sons worry her to leave the house, the judge shall enquire into her reasons and shall lay the blame on the sons, that woman shall not go out of her husband's house. If that woman has set her face to leave, the settlement which her husband gave her she shall leave to her sons, the marriage portion from her father's house she shall take and she shall marry the husband of her choice.

§ 173. If that woman where she has entered shall have borne children to her later husband after that woman has died, the former and later sons shall share her marriage portion.

§ 174. If she has not borne children to her later husband, the sons of her bridegroom shall take her marriage portion.

§ 175. If either the slave of the palace or the slave of the poor man has taken to wife the daughter of a gentleman, and she has borne sons, the owner of the slave shall have no

claim on the sons of the daughter of a gentleman for servitude.

§ 176. And if a slave of the palace or the
slave of a poor man has taken to wife the
daughter of a gentleman and, when he married
her, with a marriage portion from her father's
house she entered into the house of the slave
of the palace, or of the slave of the poor man,
and from the time that they started to keep
house and acquired property, after either the
servant of the palace or the servant of the
poor man has gone to his fate, the daughter
of the gentleman shall take her marriage
portion, and whatever her husband and she
from the time they started have acquired one
shall divide in two parts and the owner of
the slave shall take one - half, the daughter
of a gentleman shall take one-half for her
children.   If the gentleman's daughter had
no marriage portion, whatever her husband
and she from the time they started have
acquired one shall divide into two parts, and
the owner of the slave shall take half, the
gentleman's daughter shall take half for her
sons.

§ 177. If a widow whose children are young has set her face to enter into the house of another, without consent of a judge she shall not enter. When she enters into the house of another the judge shall enquire into what is left of her former husband's house, and the house of her former husband to her later husband, and that woman he shall entrust and cause them to receive a deed. They shall keep the house and rear the little ones. Not a utensil shall they give for money. The buyer that has bought a utensil of a widow's sons shall lose his money and shall return the property to its owners.

§ 178. If a lady, votary, or a vowed woman whose father has granted her a marriage portion, has written her a deed, in the deed he has written her has not, however, written her 'after her wherever is good to her to give,' has not permitted her all her choice, after the father has gone to his fate, her brothers shall take her field and her garden, and according to the value of her share shall give her corn, oil, and wool, and shall content her heart. If her brothers have not given her corn, oil, and wool according to the value of her share, and have not contented her heart, she shall give her field or her garden to a cultivator, whoever pleases her, and her cultivator shall sustain her. The field, garden, or whatever her father has given her she shall enjoy as long as she lives, she shall not give it for money, she shall not answer to another, her sonship is her brothers' forsooth.

§ 179. If a lady, a votary, or a woman vowed, whose father has granted her a marriage portion, has written her a deed, in the deed he wrote her has written her 'after her wherever is good to her to give,' has allowed to her all her choice, after the father has gone to his fate, after her wherever is good to her she shall give, her brothers have no claim on her.

§ 180. If a father to his daughter a votary, bride, or vowed woman has not granted a marriage portion, after the father has gone to his fate, she shall share in the goods of the father's house a share like one son, as long as she lives she shall enjoy, after her it is her brothers' forsooth.

§ 181. If a father has vowed to God a votary, hierodule, or NU-BAR, and has not granted her a marriage portion, after the father has gone to his fate she shall share in the goods of the father's house one-third of her sonship share and shall enjoy it as long as she lives, after her it is her brothers' forsooth.

§ 182. If a father, to his daughter, a votary of Marduk, of Babylon, has not granted her a marriage portion, has not written her a deed, after the father has gone to his fate, she shall share with her brothers in the goods of the father's house, one-third of her sonship share, and shall pay no tax; a votary of Marduk, after her, shall give wherever it is good to her.

§ 183. If a father to his daughter, a concubine, has granted her a marriage portion, has given her to a husband, has written her a deed, after the father has gone to his fate, she shall not share in the goods of the father's house.

§ 184. If a man to his daughter, a concubine, has not granted a marriage portion, has not given her to a husband, after the father has gone to his fate, her brothers according to the capacity of the father's house, shall grant her a marriage portion and shall give her to a husband.

§ 185. If a man has taken a young child 'from his waters' to sonship, and has reared him up, no one has any claim against that nursling.

§ 186. If a man has taken a young child to sonship, and when he took him his father and mother rebelled, that nursling shall return to his father's house.

§ 187. The son of a NER-SE-GA, a palace warder, or the son of a vowed woman no one has any claim upon.

§ 188. If an artisan has taken a son to bring up, and has caused him to learn his handicraft, no one has any claim.

§ 189. If he has not caused him to learn his handicraft, that nursling shall return to his father's house.

§ 190. If a man the child whom he took to

his sonship and has brought him up, has not numbered him with his sons, that nursling shall return to his father's house.

§ 191. If a man, after a young child whom he has taken to his sonship and brought him up, has made a house for himself and acquired children, and has set his face to cut off the nursling, that child shall not go his way, the father that brought him up shall give to him from his goods one-third of his sonship, and he shall go off; from field, garden, and house he shall not give him.

§ 192. If a son of a palace warder, or of a vowed woman, to the father that brought him up, and the mother that brought him up, has said 'thou art not my father, thou art not my mother,' one shall cut out his tongue.

§ 193. If a son of a palace warder, or of a vowed woman, has known his father's house, and has hated the father that brought him up or the mother that brought him up, and has gone off to the house of his father, one shall tear out his eye.

§ 194. If a man has given his son to a wet

nurse, that son has died in the hand of the wet nurse, the wet nurse without consent of his father and his mother has procured another child, one shall put her to account, and because, without consent of his father and his mother, she has procured another child, one shall cut off her breasts.

§ 195. If a man has struck his father, his hands one shall cut off.

§ 196. If a man has caused the loss of a gentleman's eye, his eye one shall cause to be lost.

§ 197. If he has shattered a gentleman's limb, one shall shatter his limb.

§ 198. If he has caused a poor man to lose his eye or shattered a poor man's limb, he shall pay one mina of silver.

§ 199. If he has caused the loss of the eye of a gentleman's servant or has shattered the limb of a gentleman's servant, he shall pay half his price.

§ 200. If a man has made the tooth of a man that is his equal to fall out, one shall make his tooth fall out.

§ 201. If he has made the tooth of a poor man to fall out, he shall pay one-third of a mina of silver.

§ 202. If a man has struck the strength of a man who is great above him, he shall be struck in the assembly with sixty strokes of a cow-hide whip.

§ 203. If a man of gentle birth has struck the strength of a man of gentle birth who is like himself, he shall pay one mina of silver.

§ 204. If a poor man has struck the strength of a poor man, he shall pay ten shekels of silver.

§ 205. If a gentleman's servant has struck the strength of a free-man, one shall cut off his ear.

§ 206. If a man has struck a man in a quarrel, and has caused him a wound, that man shall swear ' I do not strike him knowing ' and shall answer for the doctor.

§ 207. If he has died of his blows, he shall swear, and if he be of gentle birth he shall pay half a mina of silver.

§ 208. If he be the son of a poor man, he shall pay one-third of a mina of silver.

§ 209. If a man has struck a gentleman's daughter and caused her to drop what is in her womb, he shall pay ten shekels of silver for what was in her womb.

§ 210. If that woman has died, one shall put to death his daughter.

§ 211. If the daughter of a poor man through his blows he has caused to drop that which is in her womb, he shall pay five shekels of silver.

§ 212. If that woman has died, he shall pay half a mina of silver.

§ 213. If he has struck a gentleman's maid-servant and caused her to drop that which is in her womb, he shall pay two shekels of silver.

§ 214. If that maidservant has died, he shall pay one-third of a mina of silver.

§ 215. If a doctor has treated a gentleman for a severe wound with a bronze lancet and has cured the man, or has opened an abscess of the eye for a gentleman with the bronze lancet and has cured the eye of the gentleman, he shall take ten shekels of silver.

§ 216. If he (the patient) be the son of a poor man, he shall take five shekels of silver.

§ 217. If he be a gentleman's servant, the master of the servant shall give two shekels of silver to the doctor.

§ 218. If the doctor has treated a gentleman for a severe wound with a lancet of bronze and has caused the gentleman to die, or has opened an abscess of the eye for a gentleman with the bronze lancet and has caused the loss of the gentleman's eye, one shall cut off his hands.

§ 219. If a doctor has treated the severe wound of a slave of a poor man with a bronze lancet and has caused his death, he shall render slave for slave.

§ 220. If he has opened his abscess with a bronze lancet and has made him lose his eye, he shall pay money, half his price.

§ 221. If a doctor has cured the shattered limb of a gentleman, or has cured the diseased bowel, the patient shall give five shekels of silver to the doctor.

§ 222. If it is the son of a poor man, he shall give three shekels of silver.

§ 223. If a gentleman's servant, the master of the slave shall give two shekels of silver to the doctor.

§ 224. If a cow doctor or a sheep doctor has treated a cow or a sheep for a severe wound and cured it, the owner of the cow or sheep shall give one-sixth of a shekel of silver to the doctor as his fee.

§ 225. If he has treated a cow or a sheep for a severe wound and has caused it to die, he shall give a quarter of its price to the owner of the ox or sheep.

§ 226. If a brander without consent of the owner of the slave has branded a slave with an indelible mark, one shall cut off the hands of that brander.

§ 227. If a man has deceived the brander,

and has caused him to brand an indelible mark on the slave, that man one shall kill him and bury him in his house, the brander shall swear, ' Not knowing I branded him,' and shall go free.

§ 228. If a builder has built a house for a man and has completed it, he shall give him as his fee two shekels of silver *per* SAR of house.

§ 229. If a builder has built a house for a man and has not made strong his work, and the house he built has fallen, and he has caused the death of the owner of the house, that builder shall be put to death.

§ 230. If he has caused the son of the owner of the house to die, one shall put to death the son of that builder.

§ 231. If he has caused the slave of the owner of the house to die, he shall give slave for slave to the owner of the house.

§ 232. If he has caused the loss of goods, he shall render back whatever he has caused the loss of, and because he did not make strong the house he built, and it fell, from his own goods he shall rebuild the house that fell.

§ 233. If a builder has built a house for a man, and has not jointed his work, and the wall has fallen, that builder at his own cost shall make good that wall.

§ 234. If a boatman has navigated a ship of sixty *gur* for a man, he shall give him two shekels of silver for his fee.

§ 235. If a boatman has navigated a ship for a man and has not made his work trustworthy, and in that same year that he worked that ship it has suffered an injury, the boatman shall exchange that ship or shall make it strong at his own expense and shall give a strong ship to the owner of the ship.

§ 236. If a man has given his ship to a boatman, on hire, and the boatman has been careless, has grounded the ship, or has caused it to be lost, the boatman shall render ship for ship to the owner.

§ 237. If a man has hired a boatman and ship, and with corn, wool, oil, dates, or whatever it be as freight, has freighted her, that

4

boatman has been careless and grounded the ship, or has caused what is in her to be lost, the boatman shall render back the ship which he has grounded and whatever in her he has caused to be lost.

§ 238. If a boatman has grounded the ship of a man and has refloated her, he shall give money to half her price.

§ 239. If a man has hired a boatman, he shall give him six GUR of corn per year.

§ 240. If a ship that is going forward has struck a ship at anchor and has sunk her, the owner of the ship that has been sunk whatever he has lost in his ship shall recount before God, and that of the ship going forward which sunk the ship at anchor shall render to him his ship and whatever of his was lost.

§ 241. If a man has taken an ox on distraint, he shall pay one-third of a mina of silver.

§ 242. If a man has hired a working ox for one year, he shall pay four GUR of corn as its hire.

§ 243. If a milch cow, he shall give three *GUR* of corn to its owner.

§ 244. If a man has hired an ox or sheep and a lion has killed it in the open field, that loss is for its owner forsooth.

§ 245. If a man has hired an ox and through neglect or by blows has caused it to die, ox for ox to the owner of the ox he shall render.

§ 246. If a man has hired an ox and has crushed its foot or has cut its nape, ox for ox to the owner of the ox he shall render.

§ 247. If a man has hired an ox and has caused it to lose its eye, he shall pay half its price to the owner of the ox.

§ 248. If a man has hired an ox, and has crushed its horn, cut off its tail, or pierced its nostrils, he shall pay a quarter of its price.

§ 249. If a man has hired an ox, and God has struck it and it has died, the man who has hired the ox shall swear before God and shall go free.

§ 250. If a wild bull in his charge has

gored a man and caused him to die, that case has no remedy.

§ 251. If the ox has pushed a man, by pushing has made known his vice, and he has not blunted his horn, has not shut up his ox, and that ox has gored a man of gentle birth and caused him to die, he shall pay half a mina of silver.

§ 252. If a gentleman's servant, he shall pay one-third of a mina of silver.

§ 253. If a man has hired a man to reside in his field and has furnished him tools, has entrusted him the oxen and harnessed them for cultivating the field—if that man has stolen the corn or plants, and they have been seized in his hands, one shall cut off his hands.

§ 254. If he has taken the tools, worn out the oxen, from the seed which he has hoed he shall restore.

§ 255. If he has hired out the oxen of the man or has stolen the corn and has not caused it to grow in the field, that man one shall put him to account and he shall measure out sixty *GUR* of corn *per GAN* of land.

§ 256. If his compensation he is not able to pay, one shall remove the oxen from that field.

§ 257. If a man has hired a harvester, he shall give him eight *GUR* of corn per year.

§ 258. If a man has hired an ox-driver, he shall give him six *GUR* of corn per year.

§ 259. If a man has stolen a watering machine from the meadow, he shall give five shekels of silver to the owner of the watering machine.

§ 260. If he has stolen a watering bucket or a harrow, he shall pay three shekels of silver.

§ 261. If a man has hired a herdsman for the cows or a shepherd for the sheep, he shall give him eight *GUR* of corn *per annum*.

§ 262. If a man, ox, or sheep to [this section is defaced].

§ 263. If he has caused an ox or sheep which was given him to be lost, ox for ox, sheep for sheep, he shall render to their owner.

§ 264. If a herdsman who has had cows or sheep given him to shepherd, has received his hire, whatever was agreed, and his heart was contented, has diminished the cows, diminished the sheep, lessened the offspring, he shall give offspring and produce according to the tenour of his bonds.

§ 265. If a shepherd to whom cows and sheep have been given him to breed, has falsified and changed their price, or has sold them, one shall put him to account, and he shall render cows and sheep to their owner tenfold what he has stolen.

§ 266. If in a sheepfold a stroke of God has taken place or a lion has killed, the shepherd shall purge himself before God, and the accident to the fold the owner of the fold shall face it.

§ 267. If a shepherd has been careless and in a sheepfold caused a loss to take place, the shepherd shall make good the fault of the loss which he has caused to be in the fold and shall pay cows or sheep and shall give to their owner.

§ 268. If a man has hired an ox, for threshing, twenty ḴA of corn is its hire.

§ 269. If he has hired an ass, for threshing, ten ḴA of corn is its hire.

§ 270. If he has hired a calf (goat ?), for threshing, one ḴA of corn is its hire.

§ 271. If a man has hired oxen, a wagon, and its driver, he shall give one hundred and eighty ḴA of corn *per diem*.

§ 272. If a man has hired a wagon by itself, he shall give forty ḴA of corn *per diem*.

§ 273. If a man has hired a labourer, from the beginning of the year till the fifth month, he shall give six *šE* of silver *per diem*; from the sixth month to the end of the year, he shall give five *šE* of silver *per diem*.

§ 274. If a man shall hire an artisan—
    (*a*) the hire of a   . . .   five *šE* of silver
    (*b*) the hire of a brickmaker five *šE* of silver
    (*c*) the hire of a tailor   .   five *šE* of silver
    (*d*) the hire of a stone-cutter .   *šE* of silver

(*e*) the hire of a . . . . . *še* of silver
(*f*) the hire of a . . . . . *še* of silver
(*g*) the hire of a carpenter four *še* of silver
(*h*) the hire of a . . . four *še* of silver
(*i*) the hire of a . . . . . *še* of silver
(*j*) the hire of a builder . . . *še* of silver
   per diem he shall give.

§ 275. If a man has hired a (boat ?) *per diem*, her hire is three *še* of silver.

§ 276. If a man has hired a fast ship, he shall give two and a half *še* of silver *per diem* as her hire.

§ 277. If a man has hired a ship of sixty GUR, he shall give one-sixth of a shekel of silver *per diem* as her hire.

§ 278. If a man has bought a manservant or a maidservant, and he has not fulfilled his month and the *bennu* sickness has fallen upon him, he shall return him to the seller, and the buyer shall take the money he paid.

§ 279. If a man has bought a manservant or a maidservant and has a complaint, his seller shall answer the complaint.

§ 280. If a man has bought in a foreign land the manservant or the maidservant of a man, when he has come into the land and the owner of the manservant or the maidservant has recognised his manservant or his maidservant, if the manservant or maidservant are natives without price he shall grant them their freedom.

§ 281. If they are natives of another land the buyer shall tell out before God the money he paid, and the owner of the manservant or the maidservant shall give to the merchant the money he paid, and shall recover his manservant or his maidservant.

§ 282. If a slave has said to his master 'Thou art not my master,' as his slave one shall put him to account and his master shall cut off his ear.

The judgements of righteousness which Ḫammurabi the mighty king confirmed and caused the land to take a sure guidance and a gracious rule.

The following three sections, which are

known to belong to the Code from copies made for an Assyrian king in the seventh century B.C., are given here for the sake of completeness. They obviously come within the space once occupied by the five erased columns.

§ X. If a man has taken money from a merchant and has given a plantation of dates to the merchant, has said to him, 'The dates that are in my plantation take for thy money,' that merchant shall not agree, the dates that are in the plantation the owner of the plantation shall take, and he shall answer to the merchant for the money and its interests according to the tenour of his bond. The dates that are over, which are in the plantation, the owner of the plantation shall take forsooth.

§ Y. . . . the man dwelling (in the house) has given to the owner (of the house) the money of its rent in full for the year, the owner of the house has ordered the dweller to go out when his days are not full, the owner of the house, because he has ordered the dweller to leave when his days are not full, (shall give) of the money which the dweller gave him. . . .

§ Z. If a man has to pay, in money or corn, but has not money or corn to pay with, but has goods, whatever is in his hands, before witnesses, according to what he has brought, he shall give to his merchant. The merchant shall not object, he shall receive it.

INDEX

The numbers refer to the sections of the Code.

Abatement, of rent, for loss of crop, 45, 46.
    of interest, 48.
Accidental loss, by storm or deluge, falls on tenant, 45.
    shared by landlord, if before rent is paid, 46.
    by drought, storm, or deluge, postpones payment of
        debt, 48.
Adjournment, for production of witnesses, 13.
    not to exceed six months, 13.
Adoption, of natural son, 185.
    of child of living parents, 186.
    parents may object, 186.
    votary or palace official cannot object, 187.
  by artisan, 188.
      no one can reclaim child, if he has been taught handi-
        craft, 188.
      otherwise can be reclaimed, 189.
      adopted son must be formally acknowledged, 190.
      if not, returns to real parents on death of adoptive
        father, 190.
      adopted son cannot be cut off without legal process, 191.
      has one-third child's share, 191.
      but no part of estaté, 191.
      repudiation by adopted son severely punished, 192 ff.
Adultery, 129.
    penalty, drowning, 129.

Agent, relation to principal or merchant—
    must keep accounts, 100.
      of money received, 100.
      of interest due, 100.
    if unsuccessful, repays capital only, 101.
    if a loser, repays capital in full, 102.
    if robbed, can be excused payment, 103.
    must keep account of goods, 104.
    stating money value, 104.
    take inventory, 104.
    give receipt, 104.
    pays threefold for his defaults, 106.
Allotment, to ganger, constable, or tributary, 30. *See* Benefice.
Allowances, to divorced wife, 137.
    usufruct of field, garden, and goods.
Alteration of date for repayment, 48.
    called 'wetting tablet,' 48.
Approving lease, 44. *See* Lease.
Assault, of gentleman by gentleman, 202, 203.
    in a quarrel, 206.
    of poor man by poor man, 204.
    of gentleman by slave, 205.
    of pregnant woman, causing miscarriage—
        gentle woman, 209.
        poor woman, 211.
        slave, 213.
      causing her death—
        gentle woman, 210.
        poor woman, 212.
        slave, 214.
    See under Fines.
Assessment of damages—
    by sheep to growing crops, 57.
         ,,   to ripe crops, 58.
    for cutting down tree in orchard, 59.
    for not carrying out terms of lease, 42, 44.
    for assault. *See* Fines.

Assessment of damages (*contd.*)—
    for carelessness. *See* Neglect.
    for culpable lack of skill. *See* Doctor.
Assignment for debt—
    of bare field, 49.
    of corn field, 50.
    of date plantation, X.
    of crop, Y.
    of wife, child, or slave, to work off debt, 115.
Average yield, assessed damages, 42, 43, 44, 55, 62, 65.

Backbiting, 161.
Bailiff. *See* Reeve, Ganger, Constable, Benefice.
Bailment, without witness or deed—
    from domestic inferior = theft, 7.
Banishment. *See* Exile.
Bearing sentence sought to be obtained. *See* Retaliation.
Benefice, the land, house, garden, and stock—
    assigned by king to ganger, constable, or tributary, 30.
    inalienable, 32, 36, 37.
    sale, or purchase, forbidden, 35.
    price paid forfeited, 35.
    not to be exchanged, 41.
    not to be devised to females, 38.
    may be deputed, 27.
    hereditary, 28.
    forfeited, by disuse, 30.
    may not be pledged, 38.
    saleable to other official (?), 40.
Betrothed, maiden lived in father's house, 130.
Bigamy, in ignorance, 135.
Blood money. *See* Wît.
Boatmen, their duties and privileges, 234–241.
    same word denotes boat-builder (Winckler's tr.).
Boats, passenger, 276.
    freight boat, 277.
    building, 234.

Boats (*contd.*)—
>	of *60 GUR*, built, 234 (Winckler's tr.).
>	collision of, 241.
>	wreck of, 235, 236.

Bond, a written deed or contract—
>	needed for legal purchase, 7.
>	for debt, 52.
>	for storage, 122.
>	for legal marriage, 128.
>	shepherd's, 264.

Branding, brander, 226, 227.
>	on forehead, for slander, 127.
>	slave without consent of owner, 226, 227.

Brawling, in wine shop, 109.

Breach of contract—
>	by lessee, 42, 44, 256.	See Lease, Metayer, Neglect.
>	of promise, 159.

Breasts, cut off, 194.

Bride-price, a present to prospective father-in-law—
>	usually returned with wife to bridegroom, 163.
>	given back by husband to divorced wife, if not a mother, 138.
>	returned to suitor, if not accepted, 160, 161.
>	forfeited if suitor changes his mind, 159.
>	if not given back to bridegroom with wife, deducted from marriage portion repaid to father-in-law, on death of wife, without children, 164.
>	assessed at one mina of silver, for gentleman, 139.
>		„	one-third mina, for poor man, 139.
>	to be set aside for unmarried son, by his brothers, on division of father's property, 166.

Brothel (?).	See Wine shop.

Builder's duties and privileges, 228.
>	of boats, 234 (Winckler's tr.).

Burning, as penalty—
>	for votary, opening or entering wine shop, 110.
>	man and mother in incest, 157.
>	thief at fire, 25.

Business. *See* Agent, Merchant, Office.
Buyer of benefice must discharge duties, 40.

Calling to account, 42, 108, 112, 113, 116, 124, 133, 141, 194, 255, 265.
Capital suit, 3.
Captives, 133, 280.
Carrier's privileges and responsibilities, 112.
Cattle, damage *feasant pauperies*, 57.
Changeling, foisted on parents, 194.
Charges, for warehousing, 121.
    one-sixtieth value, 121.
Children. *See* Custody, Mother, Remarriage, Widow.
    born of wife remarried, under impression her husband was dead, stay with second husband, 135.
    not to dispute mother's settlement, 150.
    share equally at father's death, 165.
    reserving settlements by deed, 165.
    of second marriage to be furnished with bride-price, or portion, 166.
    of different mothers, share separately own mother's portions, 167.
    but father's property equally, 167.
    of bride and maid share equally, if latter acknowledged as sons in father's lifetime, former having preference, 170.
      otherwise, children of maid do not share, 171.
    of slave woman and free father are free, 171.
    of slave man and free mother are free, 175.
    these take half father's goods at death, 175.
Collision, 241.
Commission, trade on, 100–105. *See* Agent, Merchant.
Compensation, for eviction of tenant, Y.
    for highway robbery, 23.
Composition, for loss of life, 224.
    for bride-price, 139.
Concubine, divorced, 137.

Concubine (*contd.*)—

    not allowed, if wife provides maid, 144.

    allowed, if votary wife has no children, 145.

    not to rival wife, 145.

    father may give daughter as, 183.

    and give marriage portion, 183.

    if so, she has no share of his goods at his death, 183.

    otherwise, brothers must give her a portion, 184.

Conjugal rights, denial of, 141.

Conscript. *See* Militia.

Constable, or bailiff, runner, 36–41.

    not to depute duty, 26.

    in enforced absence on royal business, 27.

    may depute, and resume on return, 27.

    son may be deputy, 28.

    provision for child, in absence, 29.

    neglect of benefice, 30.

    three years' limit, 30.

    one year does not forfeit, 31.

    captured abroad on king's business, 32.

      to be ransomed, 32.

    benefice inalienable, 33.

    benefice protected, 34.

    not to be hired out, 35.

      plundered, 35.

      oppressed, 35.

    sale of benefice illegal, 35.

    benefice not to be exchanged, 41.

Contract. *See* Bond.

Corn land, 62.

Corporate liability, 23, 32.

Corvée. *See* Militia.

Courtship, 159, 161.

Cow, in milk, hire of, 243.

Creditor. *See also* Merchant.

    must not ill treat pledge for debt, 116.

    must release at end of three years, 117.

Creditor (*contd.*)—
    may sell pledged slave, on removal, 118.
    may not repay himself from debtor's goods, 113.
Crop, assigned for debt, 51.
    sold at king's price, 51.
Crown, man's. *See* Strength.
Cultivation of fields—
    operations needful, 43.
Custody of child, in mother, 29.
Cutting down trees—
    assessment of damage, half mina of silver per tree, 59.

Damage to crops, by sheep—
    assessed at twenty GUR per GAN, 57.
    to ripe crops, at sixty GUR per GAN, 58.
    by flooding field, 56.
    by cutting down trees, assessed at half mina of silver per
        tree, 59.
Damages, for breach of contract, 42, 44.
    for eviction from purchase, 12.
    for eviction from house, Y.
Damnum sine injuria, 115, 118, 123, 250.
Date palm, plantation of, X.
Daughter cannot inherit benefice, 38.
Death penalty, inflicted for—
    witchcraft, 1.
    threatening witnesses, 3.
    perjury, 3.
    theft, 4.
    receiving stolen goods, 4.
    buying from domestic inferior, 7.
    taking on deposit from domestic inferior, 7.
    in default of multiple restitution, for theft of second
        order, 8.
    appropriation of lost property, 9.
    selling lost property, 10.
    vexatious claim of property as lost, 11.

Death penalty (*contd.*)—

 kidnapping, 14.

 procuring desertion of slave, 15.

 harbouring fugitive slave, 18.

   „ of defaulting militia, 16.

 detaining fugitive slave, 18.

 keeping recaptured slave, 19.

 housebreaking, 21.

 highway robbery, 22.

 theft at fire, 25.

 allowing seditious brawling in wine shop, 109.

 rape of betrothed maiden, 130.

 for ganger, constable, neglecting duty, 26.

   „   „ sending substitutes, 26.

 causing death of pregnant woman by assault, 210.

 for getting a slave branded unknown to owner, 227.

 for building so badly as to cause death of owner, 229.

 See also Burning, Drowning, Impalement.

Death of defendant, 12.

Debt, abatement for damage by storm, deluge, and drought, 48.

 not to be repaid from debtor's goods, without his consent, 113.

 hostages for, 117.

 to be well treated, 118.

 released after three years, 117.

 of man before marriage, not binding on wife, 151.

 of woman before marriage, not binding on husband, 151.

 of both after marriage, binding on both, 151.

Debtor's risk, 48.

 privileged to pay in kind, Z.

Defamation, 161.

Deferred foreclosure, 48.

Degradation from office, 5.

Deification of river Euphrates, 2.

Delegatus non potest delegare, 26, 33.

Deposit. *See* Storage, Trust, Warehouse, 7.

Deposit (*contd.*)—

    not recoverable unless witnessed and sealed for, 123.

    from domestic inferior, illegal without witnessed contract, 7.

Desertion, by husband, of wife—

    involuntary, 133.

    of city and wife, 136.

    of adoptive parents, 193.

Detention of fugitive slave punished, 19.

Disinheritance, for incest, 159.

    of son, 168.

    not without legal process and for good cause, 168.

Distraint for debt, 114, 115.

    unjustified, fine one-third mina of silver, each time, 114.

    death of person taken in, 115, 116.

    not allowed on warehoused goods, 120.

    of working ox fined, 241.

District liable, for highway robbery, 23.

    for ransom of official, 32.

Diverted to, perhaps 'captured in,' Winckler's tr.

Divorce, 137, 138.

    wife takes her bride-price, 137.

    or fixed sum, one mina of silver from gentleman, 139.

    or fixed sum, one-third mina from poor man, 140.

Doctor, privileges and responsibilities, 215–221.

    fees for cures, 215, 221.

    causes death, 218–220.

    paid by assailant, 206.

Domestic inferior. *See* Minor.

Dowry. *See* Bride-price.

Drowning, as penalty for—

    selling drink too cheap, 109.

    adultery, 129.

    bad wife, 143.

    incest with daughter-in-law, 155.

Drowning, as penalty for (*contd.*)—
> deserting husband's house in his enforced absence, being
> > provided with proper maintenance, 133.
Dyke, 53.

Ear cut off as penalty, 205.
Endowment of office. *See* Benefice.
Equals, assault of, 200, 203, 206.
Evicted purchaser reimbursed, 9.
> tenant reimbursed, Y.
Exchange, of benefice illegal, 41.
Exile, penalty for incest, 154.
Eye, torn out as penalty, 193.
> struck out in assault, 196.
> disease of, 215.
> cure of, fee for, ten shekels of silver, 215.
> loss of eye, assessed at five shekels of silver, 220.

False judgement, penalty for, 5.
> claims for money or goods, 106, 107, 126.
> accusation of adultery, 131.
Farm. *See* Lease.
Fatal assault of gentleman by gentleman, 207.
> of gentleman by poor man, 208.
Favourite son, may be gifted by father, 165.
> in his lifetime, 165.
> by written deed, 165.
> other children no claim against, 165.
> takes equal share with them on father's death, 165.
Fees for curing wound, or disease of eye, by surgical operation—
> gentleman pays ten shekels of silver, 215.
> poor man pays five shekels of silver, 216.
> slave pays two shekels of silver, 216.
> cure of broken limb or diseased bowel—
> > gentleman pays five shekels, 221.
> > poor man pays three shekels, 222.
> > slave pays two shekels, 223.

Fees (*contd.*)—

    cure of bad wound of ox or sheep, one-sixth of shekel, 224.

    for building house, two shekels *per SAR*, 228.

    to boatman for navigating boat, two shekels, 234.

    warehousing goods, one-sixtieth value, 121.

Fines imposed for—

    unlawful distraint, one-third mina, 114.

    seducing daughter-in-law before marriage, half mina, 156.

    aggravated assault, gentleman on gentleman, one mina, 203.

    aggravated assault, poor man on poor man, ten shekels, 204.

    fatal wound in quarrel, gentleman to gentleman, half mina, 207.

    fatal wound in quarrel, poor man to poor man, third mina, 208.

    assault on pregnant gentlewoman, causing miscarriage, ten shekels, 209.

    assault on pregnant poor woman, causing miscarriage, five shekels, 211.

    assault on pregnant slave, causing miscarriage, two shekels, 213.

    assault on pregnant poor woman, causing her death, half mina, 212.

    assault on pregnant slave, causing her death, third mina, 214.

    causing death of ox or sheep, by careless operation, quarter price, 225.

    distraint on working ox, one-third mina, 241.

    mutilation of hired ox, quarter price, 248.

    letting vicious ox gore a man to death, half mina, 251.

    stealing corn or plants, on metayer, sixty *GUR* of corn *per GAN*, 255.

    letting oxen, taken on metayer, sixty *GUR* of corn *per GAN*, 255.

    theft of watering machine, five shekels, 259.

Fines imposed on (*contd.*)—
    theft of water bucket, or plough (harrow?), three shekels,
        260.
    (*N.B.*—Fines reckoned in silver, 60 shekels to the mina.)
Fires, theft at, 25.
Floods, 45, 46, 48.
Forfeit of price paid in illegal purchase, 35, 37, 177.
    oxen and field, for neglect to cultivate, 256.
Forfeiture of claim—
    by self-help, 113.
    by cruelty, 116.
Fortress of the king, may be 'defeat of the king,' Winckler's tr.
Foster mother, duties and liabilities, 194.
Freedom, of hostage for debt, after three years, 117.
    to marry, as she chooses, on part of divorced wife, after
        bringing up children, 137.
    daughter-in-law, seduced before marriage, 158.
    widow, leaving settlement to children, 172.
Free-men sold into slavery, to pay fine, 54.
Fugitive, slave, 16, 17.
    poor man, 16.

Ganger, associated with constable, *q.v.*
Gentleman, one of three estates, contrasted with poor man
    and slave, 196, 197, 199, etc.
Gift. *See* Favourite son.
Goring by ox, 250, 251.
Gouging out eye, 196.
    penalty, 196, 198.
Governor, duties and liabilities, 23, 33 ff.
    not to delegate duty, 34.
    nor accept substitute, 34.
    not to oppress subordinates, 35.
Granary, 113.
Guilty knowledge, by buyer of stolen goods, 10.

Hand of God, 45, 46, 48.

Hands cut off, penalty for—
    striking father, 195.
    causing death by careless operation on free-man, 218.
    branding slave, without owner's knowledge, 226.
Harbouring, fugitive slave, 16.
    militiaman, or conscript, 16.
Herdsmen. *Sée* Shepherds.
Highway robbery, 22. *See* Robbery.
Hire, of land, house, garden. *See* Lease.
    scale fixed by king, 44, 51.
    wages fixed for—

boatman,	6 *GUR* of corn *per annum*,		239.
working ox,	4	,, ,,	242.
cow in milk, (?)	3	,, ,,	243.
reaper	8	,, ,,	257.
thresher	6	,, ,,	258.
herdman, or shepherd,	8	,, ,,	261.
ox, for threshing,	20 *KA* of corn *per diem*,		268.
ass, for threshing,	10	,, ,,	269.
calf, for threshing,	1 *KA*	,, ,,	270.
oxen, wagon, and driver,	180	,, ,,	271.
wagon alone,	40	,, ,,	272.
labourer, first five months,	6 *ŠE* silver	,,	273.
,, last seven months,	5	,, ,,	273.
artisan,	5	,, ,,	274.
brickmaker,	5	,, ,,	274.
tailor,	5	,, ,,	274.
stone cutter,	5 (?)	,, ,,	274.
milkman,	5	,, ,,	274.
carpenter,	4	,, ,,	274.
a *SA*,	4	,, ,,	274.
boat,	3	,, ,,	275.
passenger boat,	2½	,, ,,	276.
freight boat of 60 *GUR*,	⅙ shekel	,,	277.

    (*N.B.*—In corn measure, 1 *GUR*=300 *KA*, worth one
      shekel of silver, and one shekel=180 *ŠE*.
Hostage for debt. *See* Mancipium.

Housebreaking, 21, 125.
Husband. *See* Re-marriage, Wife, Divorce, Separation.
Hypothecation, of crop, regulated, 49.

Identification of lost property, 9.
Ignorance, plea of, 206, 227. *See* Scienter.
Illegal purchase, 35, 37.
Impalement, as penalty, 153.
    for procuring husband's death, 153.
Incest, 154–158.
    of man and daughter, 154.
    of man and daughter-in-law, 155, 156.
    of man and mother, 157.
    of man and stepmother, 158.
Inheritance. *See* Share.
Innocent wife, separation from bad husband, 142. *See* Separation.
Interest on loan, etc., 49, 50, 100, X.
    abatement, 48.
Intimidation of witnesses, 3.

Jilting, 159.
Judge, duties and liabilities, 5, 9, 127, 167, 168, 172, 177.
Judgement, false. *See* False.
    by default, 10.

Kidnapping, 14.
King's standard, 44, 51. *See* Hire, Scale.

Lancet, bronze, used in surgical operations, 215, 218, 220.
Landlord's risks, 46.
Lease, of house, Y.
    field to cultivate, 42.
      ,, to reclaim, three years, 44.
      ,, to plant as garden, five years, 60.
    garden to till, 64.
    terms, not invalidated by neglect, 52.

Lease (*contd.*)—
 damages for not carrying out terms, 63.
 See Metayer.
Levy. *See* Militia.
Lex talionis. *See* Retaliation.
Libel. *See* Slander.
Lion, referred to, 244, 266.
Local liability for—
 compensation for highway robbery, 23, 24.
 redemption of captive official, 32.
Loss, by burglary or rebellion, 125.
 of hired animal, by lion, 244.
   ,,   by neglect, 245.
   ,,   by blows, 245.
   ,,   by hand of God, 249.
 of flock or herd, by hand of God, 266.
   ,,   by lion, 226.
 of crop, when shared by landlord, 45.
 of interest. *See* Abatement.
Lost property, recovery by owner, 9.
 sale by finder = theft, 9.
Lying, 11, 12.

Magistrate, over township, 23, 24.
Maid, female slave—
 given by wife to husband, to bear children, 144.
 not to rival mistress, 146.
 if so, reckoned slave again, 146.
 not sold, if a mother, 146.
 may be sold, if not, 146.
 children, acknowledged by husband, in his lifetime, share
  equally with wife's children, 170.
 otherwise, free, but not heirs, 171.
Maintenance, of wife in absence, 133–135.
 of divorced wife, 137.
 or concubine, 137.
Malice prepense, 206.

Malicious abuse of process, 12.

Mancipium, hostage to work off debt—
    natural death, 115.
    done to death, 116.
    free after three years, if free born, 117.
    slave, can be sold, by creditor on removal, 118.
        but not if mother of debtor's children, 119.
        redeemed by debtor, 119.

Mansion, 'great house.' *See* Palace.

Manslaughter, of mancipium, 116.
    if slave, penalty one-third mina of silver, 116.
    by blow in quarrel, 207, 208.

Marks, on slave. *See* Branding.

Marriage portion, given by father to bride—
    returned on divorce, 137.
    not to bad wife, 141.
    returned to injured wife, 142.
       „   to invalid wife, who leaves husband, 149.
    property of wife's children, 162.
    father of bride cannot reclaim, if she has children of the marriage, 162.
    returned, if wife dies childless, 163.
    less bride-price, if not repaid to husband, 164.
    if wife re-marry, shared by children of both marriages, 173.
    taken by children of first marriage, if none of second, 174.
    free wife of slave, takes her marriage portion, if any on his death, for self and children, 175.

Master's right over married slave's property, 175, 176.
    pays for slave's cure, 217, 223. *See* Slave.

Merchant, trader, relations with agent, 100–107.
    official (?), 40.
    as creditor, money-lender, 40, 49, 116, 118, 119, 152, X, Z.
    bound to accept goods, for money or corn, Z.
    pays fivefold for overcharging agent, 107.
    likely to change residence, 118.

Metayer, system of lease, landlord finds seed, implements, working animals, etc. *See* also Lease, 253.

Militia, or conscript, for *corvée*—
 fugitive from, 9.
 granted to governor, 33.

Minor, status of, 7.

Miscarriage, 209. *See* Assault, Fine.

Money, not sealed for, cannot enter account, 105. *See* Hire, Price, Fines.

Mortgage. *See* Debt.

Mortgagor's power of sale, 118.
 option to refuse foreclosure, X.

Mother, has custody of children, 29.
 incest with, 157.

Mutilation, as penalty. *See* Branding, Ear, Eye, Hands, Breasts, Tongue.
 of hired ox, 248.
 either punishment of offending member, or retaliation
  for mutilation. *See* Retaliation.

Neglect, to cultivate field leased, 42, 43.
 to reclaim field leased, 44.
 to set up dwelling, 47.
 to strengthen dyke, 53.
 to plant garden leased, 61–63.
 to till garden, 65.
 to build house properly, 232.
 to cultivate on metayer, 253.
 to confine vicious ox, 251, 252.

Oath, in legal process. *See* Sworn Deposition 9.
 for purgation, 20, 131, 227, 266.
 as to loss, 23, 103, 126, 240, 249.
 as to deposit, 120.
 as to injury, 206.

Office, duty of official, 40.

Officials, *PA-PA* and *NU-TUR*—
  duties and liabilities, 33, 34.   *See* Governor, Ganger,
    Constable, Reeve, Bailiff, Runner, Palace, Judge.
Ordeal, by water, nature of, 2.
  for witchcraft, 2.
  purgation of slander, 132.
Ox, working, not to be distrained on, 241.
    „   hire, 242.
  furious, 250.
  vicious, 251.

Palace, equivalent to state, king, gentleman's residence—
  property of, 11.
  ransom by, 32.
  place of judgement, 109.
Palace official, 'one who stands in the presence'—
  child of, may be adopted without demur, 192.
Perjury, 3, 4.
Personal property of official pledged, 39.
Pin-money. *See* Settlement.
Pledge, of benefice, illegal, 38.
  personal property allowed, 39. *See* Debt.
Poor man, separate estate, contrasted with gentleman and
  slave—
    theft from, 8.
    abduction of slave from, 15.
    liable to conscription or levy, 16.
    reduced charges for divorce, 140.
    owned slave, 15, 175, 176.
    his eye or limb valued at one mina of silver, 198.
    his tooth valued at one-third mina of silver, 201.
    assault by poor man, 204.
    assault by, 208.
    fee for cure of wound or eye, 208.
    fee for cure of limb or bowel, 222.
Pregnant woman. *See* Assault, Fine.
Prescriptive right to benefice acquired by discharge of office, 30.

Presumption, 7.
Price of drink not to be less than corn, 108.
    except at harvest time, then five-sixths, 111.
Principal. *See* Merchant.
Procuration of desertion of slave from master, 15.
Produce rent, 42.
    of field, one-half or one-third crop, 46.
    of garden, two-thirds crop, 64.

Ransom, of captive official, 32.
    by serf, 32.
    by town, 32.
    by palace, 32.
Rape, of betrothed maiden, 130.
Rebellion, loss by, 125.
Receipt, sealed written document—
    to be taken by agent for goods committed, 104.
    to be taken by depositor, 124, 125.
Receiving of stolen goods, 10.
Reclaiming lease, 44.
Recovery, of lost property, 9, 10, 126.
    of deposit, 124, 125.
Redemption of pledge or mancipium, 119.
    debtor must redeem a maid who has borne him children, 119.
Reeve. *See* Ganger.
Referees. *See* Witnesses.
Refusal to name owner, 19.
    of conjugal rights, 141.
Reimbursement to evicted purchaser, 9.
Re-marriage of divorced woman, 141.
    of widow, 173.
    her marriage portion shared equally by children of both marriages, 173.
    if no children of second marriage, those of first take all, 174
Remission of penalty, 129.

Rents, usually share of produce, 46, 64.
    fixed by Code for—
        land leased to be reclaimed, three years free, fourth
            year ten *GUR per GAN*, 44 ; cf. 63.
        land leased to plant as garden, four years free, fifth
            year half-produce, 60 ; cf. Lev. xix. 25.
        garden leased to till, two-thirds produce, 64.
        abatement, if crop destroyed, 45.
        no abatement if culpable negligence, 52.
Repatriation of slave, 280, 281.
Repudiation of adoptive parents—
    by son of votary, or palace official, 192.
Res perit domino, 115.
Restitution, compensation, damages, reimbursement—
    simple, 9, 10, 12.
    goods for goods, 232.
    ox or ass, for same, 245, 246, 263.
    slave for slave, 219, 231.
    of deposit, 125.
    threefold, for cheating principal, 106.
    fivefold, for goods lost or stolen by carrier, 112 ; cf. 12.
    sixfold, for over-charging agent, 107.
    tenfold, for theft by poor man, 8.
        ,,   for culpable loss by herdsman or shepherd, 265.
    twelvefold, for false sentence by judge, 5.
    thirtyfold, for theft by gentleman, 5.
Retaliation, eye for eye, 196.
    limb for limb, 197.
    tooth for tooth, 200.
    son for son, 116, 230.
    slave for slave, 219, 231.
    suitor to bear penalty he sought to bring, 4, 13.
    See Restitutions.
Return, of slave purchased—
    permissible within one month, for disease, 278.
    or other undisclosed defect, 279.
Reward, for capturing fugitive slave, 17.

Risks, landlord's, 45, 46.
 lessor's, 244.
 warehouseman's, 125.
 tenant's, 45.
Robbery, 22, 23.
Runnel, 55.
Runner. *See* Constable.

Sacrilegious theft—
 of first order, 6.
 of second order, 8.
Sale of, man and property, to pay fine, 54.
 wife or child, for debt, 117.
 crops to pay, according to scale, 51.
Scale damages. *See* King's standard.
Scandal, 132.
Scourging, with cowhide whip, sixty strokes, 202.
Second marriage, 166, 167. *See* Re-marriage, Widow.
Seduction, of betrothed daughter-in-law, 155.
 of slave, from service, 15.
Self-help, forbidden, 113.
Separation, of husband and wife—
 grounds for, on part of husband—
  gone out, deserted home, 142.
  belittled wife, 142.
 on part of wife—
  set to desert home, 141.
  quarrelsome, 141.
  ruinous, 141.
  belittled husband, 141.
Settlement, or pin-money, estate, or goods settled on wife—
 by husband, in lifetime, by written deed, 150.
 children not to dispute, 150.
 wife has freedom of testamentary devise, 150.
 among her children of that marriage, 150.
 wife may not leave to brothers, 150.

Settlement (*contd.*)—

 widow enjoys for life, if she remains in husband's house, 171.

 widow bequeaths to children, 171.

  ,, resigns if she re-marries, 172.

 compare gift to favourite child.

Share, of father's property, on his death—

 equally by all children, 165.

 divorced wife, as one child, 137.

 with reservation apart, of gift to favourite, 165.

  ,, ,, of wife's settlement, 150.

  ,, ,, bride-price for unmarried son, 166.

  ,, ,, portion for votary sister, 178.

 of mother's marriage portion, on her death, 167.

 all her children equally, 167.

 children of second wife share own mother's portion, 167.

 children of both mothers share equally in father's property, 167.

 children of maid, if acknowledged, share equally with children of wife, latter taking precedence, 170.

Shepherds, duties and liabilities of, 262–267.

Slander, against votary or married woman, 127.

 of wife, 132.

 of suitor, 161.

 judiciary, against referees, 3.

 of title, 11.

 liability for, passively transmitted, 12.

 seditious, 109.

Slave, one of three estates, domestic inferior—

 not free to contract except by deed and bond, 6.

 seduction from service, penal, 15.

 fugitive, harbouring, 16.

  ,, capturing, 17.

  ,, retaining, 19.

  ,, refuses to name owner, 18.

  ,, re-escape of captured, 20.

 subject to levy, 16.

Slave (*contd.*)—

    marries free woman, 175.

    children free, 175.

    woman marries master, bears sons, not to be sold, 119.

    cure of, paid for by master, 218, 223.

    his eye or limb, valued at half-price, 199.

    assault on free-man by slave, 205.

    gored by ox, 251.

    of poor man, 219.

    captured and repatriated, 280.

    freed, if native, 281.

    rebellious, repudiates master, 282.

Speculation in crops, futures, discouraged, 49, 50, X.

Spell, magical. *See* Witchcraft.

Stay of case, for production of witnesses, 13.

Stolen goods, guilty purchase of = theft, 10.

Storage. *See* Warehouse, Deposit.

Strength of a man, crown of the head (?), genitalia—

    penalty for wounding the, of—

        superior, 202.

        equal, 203.

        poor man, 204.

        free-man by slave, 205.

Striking or wounding. *See* Assaults.

    of father by son, 195.

Sub-letting, not to be objected to, 47.

Subornation, of perjury, 4.

Summons to appear before judge, 127. *See* Calling to account.

Superior, assault of, 202.

Surgeon. *See* Doctor.

Sworn deposition, 9, 23, 103, 120, 126, 206, 240, 249.

Tablet, broken, annulment of contract, 37.

    wetted, to rewrite date, 48.

Temple, property protected, 6, 8.

    bound to ransom captive, 32.

Tenant's risks, 45.

Theft, first order, involving entry, 6.
    second order, in the open, 8.
    by keeping property found, 9.
    by selling property found, 10.
    aggravated at fire, 25.
    from deposit, 120.
        under metayer, 254.   *See* Bailment, Lost property,
            Sacrilegious, Stolen goods, Treasonable, Receiving.

Threatening witnesses, 3.

Threshing floor, 113.

Tongue cut out, 192.

Treasonable theft, first order, 6.
    second order, 8.

Trespass, to realty, 54.
    dolus, 54.
    culpa, 55.

Tributary, a beneficed person, paid tribute, 36–41.
    benefice inalienable, 36.   *See* Benefice.

Trust, deposit, regulated—
    corn in granary, 120.
    any goods, 122.

Undertaking.   *See* Lease.

Untitled possession, 9, 10.

Veterinary surgeon, duties and liabilities of, 224, 225.

Vexatious claim of property as lost, 11.

Vivum vadium, 49.

Votary, not to open or enter wine shop, 110.
    protected from slander, 127.
    as wife, 145.
    gives maid to husband, to bear children, 146.
    not to be rivalled by maid, 147.
    dowered as for marriage, 178.
    free to leave her portion, if allowed by father's deed, 178,
        179.

Votary (*contd.*)—

> otherwise, brothers assume charge of her estate and main-
> tain her, 178.
>
> or if they do not content her, she farms it out, 178.
>
> if father gives her no portion, entitled on his death to
> one child's share, 180.
>
> but must leave to brothers, 180.
>
> if dedicated by father, and not portioned, entitled to one-
> third share at his death, 181.
>
> must leave this to brethren, 181.
>
> if dedicated by father to Marduk of Babylon, and not
> portioned, entitled to one-third share at his death,
> 182.
>
> pays no taxes, 182.
>
> leaves property as she likes, 182.
>
> her child may be adopted, without her consent, 193.
>
> „ if adopted, severely punished for repudiating
> adopted parents, 193.
>
> usually lived in convent, 110.
>
> cannot alienate or mortgage estate, 178.
>
> unless power granted by father's deed, 179.
>
> when brothers cannot interfere, 179.

Wages. *See* Hire.

Warden. *See* Constable.

Wards, children of re-married widow, by first marriage,
177.

Warehousing, 120–126.

> fee for, one-sixtieth value, 121.
>
> liability for loss in warehouse, 125.

Waste, 59.

> land. *See* Reclaiming lease, 44, 63.

Weights, great, 108.

Widow, on husband's death—

> stays in his house, 171.
>
> takes her portion and settlement, 171.
>
> may not alienate them from children, 171.

Widow (*contd.*)—

    if no settlement, takes portion, and one child's share, 172.

    children cannot turn her out without legal process, 172.

    if she wishes to leave and re-marry, resigns settlement to children, but takes portion, 172.

    on her death, children of both marriages divide her portion equally, 172.

    with young children, may marry, but she and husband are bound trustees for the children, 177.

Wife, of free-man, not to be slandered, 127.

    not legally married, without bonds, 128.

    adultery by, drowned, 129.

    falsely accused, 131.

    slandered, 132.

    of captive husband, 133–135.

    bound to preserve fidelity if provided for, 133.

    otherwise, may re-marry, 134.

    but must rejoin husband, on return, 135.

    children, of second marriage, if any, stay with father, 135.

    deserted, 136.

    divorce of, who has borne children, 137.

    divorced, takes marriage portion, usufruct of field, garden, and property, only leaves house, has custody and education of children, then takes one child's share, and is free to re-marry, 137.

        ,,   and if not a mother, takes marriage portion and bride-price, 138.

        ,,   or in lieu of bride-price, fixed sum, 139, 140.

    may seek divorce, 141.

    bad, divorced without compensation, 141.

        ,, reduced to status of slave, 141.

    denies conjugal rights, 142.

    if bad, drowned, 143.

    if justified by husband's cruelty, separated, 142.

Wife (*contd.*)—

> good, stays at home, is not quarrelsome, economical, does not belittle her husband, has no vice, 142.
>
> may give maid to husband to bear children, 144.
>
> husband then may not take concubine, 144.
>
> maid may not rival, 145.
>
> childless, does not give maid, husband can take concubine, 145.
>
> concubine not to rival, 145.
>
> invalid, to be maintained, not divorced, 148.
>
>   „   husband can marry second wife, 148.
>
>   „   may leave husband, taking portion, 149.
>
> second wife only allowed, if first be invalid, or divorced, 137–141, 148.
>
> can leave settlement to any child she prefers, 150.
>
> liability for husband's debts, 151.
>
> procuring death of husband, for love of another, impaled, 153.
>
> of official, no claim on benefice, 38.
>
> deserted, free to marry, 136.

Wine seller, duties and liabilities, 108–110.

> not to sell drink cheaper than corn, 108.
>
> relaxation of this rule, 111.
>
> not to suffer brawling or seditious talk, 109.
>
> bound to hale brawlers to palace, 109.
>
> votary not to be, 110.

Wît, 24, 116.

Witchcraft, laws against, 1, 2.

Witnesses—

> (1) referees, elders of township, assessors of judge.
>
> (2) knowing facts, recognising property.
>
> (3) to document.
>
> penalty for threatening, death, 3.
>
>   „   bribing, to bear sentence, 4.
>
> necessary for legal purchase, 7, 9.
>
> time granted to produce, 13.

Witnesses (*contd.*)—
    to deposit, 122.
    knowing lost property, 9.
Working expenses, 49.
Wounds, given in quarrel, 206.
    grievous, cure by doctor, 215, 217, 218.
    to cattle, cure, 225.

PRINTED BY MORRISON AND GIBB LIMITED, EDINBURGH

A GREAT BIBLICAL ENCYCLOPÆDIA.

NOW COMPLETE.

'The standard authority for biblical students of the present generation.'—*Times.*

In Four Volumes, imperial 8vo (of nearly 900 pages each).
Price per Volume, in cloth, 28s.; in half morocco, 34s.,

A DICTIONARY OF THE BIBLE,

Dealing with its Language, Literature, and Contents, including the Biblical Theology.

Edited by JAMES HASTINGS, M.A., D.D., with the Assistance of J. A.
SELBIE, D.D., and, chiefly in the Revision of the Proofs, of the late
A. B. DAVIDSON, D.D., LL.D., Edinburgh; S. R. DRIVER, D.D.,
Litt.D., Oxford; and H. B. SWETE, D.D., Litt.D., Cambridge.

*Full Prospectus, with Specimen Pages, from all Booksellers, or
from the Publishers.*

'We offer Dr. Hastings our sincere congratulations on the publication of the first
instalment of this great enterprise. . . . A work was urgently needed which should
present the student with the approved results of modern inquiry, and which should
also acquaint him with the methods by which theological problems are now approached
by the most learned and devout of our theologians.'—*Guardian.*

'We welcome with the utmost cordiality the first volume of Messrs. Clark's great
enterprise, "A Dictionary of the Bible." That there was room and need for such a
book is unquestionable. . . . We have here all that the student can desire, a work of
remarkable fulness, well up to date, and yet at the same time conservative in its
general tendency, almost faultlessly accurate, and produced by the publishers in a most
excellent and convenient style. We can thoroughly recommend it to our readers as a
book which should fully satisfy their anticipations. . . . This new Dictionary is one of
the most important aids that have recently been furnished to a true understanding of
Scripture, and, properly used, will brighten and enrich the pulpit work of every
minister who possesses it. . . . We are greatly struck by the excellence of the short
articles. They are better done than in any other work of the kind. We have compared
several of them with their sources, and this shows at once the unpretentious labour
that is behind them. . . . Dr. A. B. Davidson is a tower of strength, and he shows at his
best in the articles on Angels, on Covenant (a masterpiece, full of illumination), and on
Eschatology of the Old Testament. His contributions are the chief ornaments and
treasure-stores of the Dictionary. . . . We are very conscious of having done most
inadequate justice to this very valuable book. Perhaps, however, enough has been said
to show our great sense of its worth. It is a book that one is sure to be turning to again
and again with increased confidence and gratitude. It will be an evil omen for the
Church if ministers do not come forward to make the best of the opportunity now
presented them.'—EDITOR, *British Weekly.*

'Will give widespread satisfaction. Every person consulting it may rely upon its
trustworthiness. . . . Far away in advance of any other Bible Dictionary that has ever
been published in real usefulness for preachers, Bible students, and teachers.'—
Methodist Recorder.

'This monumental work. It has made a great beginning, and promises to take
rank as one of the most important biblical enterprises of the century.'—*Christian
World.*

EDINBURGH: T. & T. CLARK, 38 GEORGE STREET.

Just published, in post 8vo, Fourth Edition, Revised and Enlarged,
price 6s.,

THE
MIRACLES OF UNBELIEF.

BY THE

Rev. FRANK BALLARD, M.A., B.Sc., London.

CONTENTS.—Introductory—The Attitude of the Christian Church
—Statement of the Case—The Realm of Physical Science—
Facts of History and their Explanation—The Realm of
Psychology—The Moral Realm—Christ: His Origin and
Character—The Spiritual Realm—Complication, Culmination,
Conclusion—Special Note on Haeckel's 'Riddle of the Uni-
verse'—Appendix—Index.

'From beginning to end of the book there is not a single dull passage,
not a sentence obscure from overloading, not an argument skimped into
shallowness, not a point ineffectively put. . . . The interest never flags;
one is carried from point to point by perspicuous links of connection till
all are welded together into a complete and rounded whole. . . . It is a
perfect mine of quotation for men with little time for deep study, who
are called, as modern ministers are, to be not only visitors and workers,
but also preachers and teachers.'—*Guardian.*

'A most useful volume, thoroughly up to date, clear and telling in
style and thought, and very well informed.'—*British Weekly.*

'By all odds the best apology of the Christian religion that has
appeared for many a day.'—*Presbyterian and Reformed Review.*

'This is a well-written, reasonable, forcible piece of argument. We
have been much impressed by Mr. Ballard's earnestness and acumen; his
book is a real contribution to the large literature of Apologetics.'—
Christian World.

EDINBURGH: T. & T. CLARK, 38 George Street.
London: SIMPKIN, MARSHALL, HAMILTON, KENT, & CO. LIMITED.

Now ready, in crown 8vo, price 2s.,

HEBREW IDEALS.

FROM THE STORY OF THE PATRIARCHS.

A Study of Old Testament Faith and Life.

BY

Rev. JAMES STRACHAN, M.A.

This handbook gives, not a critical analysis of documents, but a sympathetic interpretation of ideals.

CONTENTS. — Ideals — Separation — Blessedness — Worship — Truth—Decision—Warfare—Peace—Assurance—Grace— Patience—Compassion—Power—Hospitality—Education —Intercession—Mercy—Judgment—Integrity—Laughter —Tears—Aspiration—Discipline—Sacrifice—Pilgrimage —Love—Heaven.

'Clear in style, rich in thought, full of reverence for the Hebrew ideal.'—*Aberdeen Free Press.*

'An able and charming book. . . . The style is incisive, the treatment reverent and philosophical. . . . It is just the book needed, and should be in every teachers' and Sunday-school library.'—*Methodist Sunday-school Record.*

EDINBURGH : T. & T. CLARK, 38 GEORGE STREET.

LONDON : SIMPKIN, MARSHALL, HAMILTON, KENT, & CO. LIMITED.